Puffin Books

THE MIDNIGHT FEAST JOKE BOOK

This book of jokes has been cooked up
to make you laugh and titter,
so should you turn bananas,
make sure you're not a fritter!

If you should fancy a midnight munch
delve into this feast of fun.
But mind you don't have a fit of the giggles,
and choke on your iced bun!

The MIDNIGHT FEAST Joke Book

Shoo Rayner

PUFFIN BOOKS

PUFFIN BOOKS

Published by the Penguin Group
Penguin Books Ltd, 27 Wrights Lane, London W8 5TZ, England
Penguin Books USA Inc., 375 Hudson Street, New York, New York 10014, USA
Penguin Books Australia Ltd, Ringwood, Victoria, Australia
Penguin Books Canada Ltd, 10 Alcorn Avenue, Toronto, Ontario, Canada M4V 3B2
Penguin Books (NZ) Ltd, 182–190 Wairau Road, Auckland 10, New Zealand

Penguin Books Ltd, Registered Offices: Harmondsworth, Middlesex, England

First published 1993
10 9 8 7 6 5 4 3 2

The moral right of the author has been asserted

Filmset in Times 14/15 pt

Typeset by DatIX International Limited, Bungay, Suffolk
Printed in England by Clays Ltd, St Ives plc

INGREDIENTS

ANIMAL CRACKERS

My sister does
bird impressions.
She eats worms!

Why do giraffes have long necks?
Because a little goes a long way!

What do parrots eat?
Polly filler!

What did the dog say to the bone?
It's nice gnawing you!

I've got a bone to pick with you!

What do geese eat?
Gooseberries!

What is a hedgehog's
favourite meal?
Prickled onions!

What
is big,
red
and eats
rocks?

*A big
red
rock
eater!*

What would you call the
last rabbit in Wales?
A Welsh Rarebit!

What would you call a
cat that has eaten a duck?
A duck-filled fatty puss!

Pardon!

If a dog eats garlic,
does that make his
bark worse than his bite?

If your pet alligator
is green, why do
you call him Ginger?
Because he snaps!

How do you spell a hungry
horse in only four letters?
M.T.G.G.

What's white on the outside
and green on the inside?
A frog sandwich!

What do frogs make
beer from?
Hops!

What goes
dot dot
ribbet ribbet
dash dash?
Morse toad!

What do frogs
like to drink?
Croaka-Cola!

Why do bees have
sticky hair?
*Because they
use honey combs!*

✳ **Advertisement Feature** ✳

Why did you eat all the
white meat off the chicken?
  To make a clean breast of it!

What happened to the
chicken that had a hot bath?
  It laid hard-boiled eggs!

What do you get if you cross a
chicken with a cement mixer?
  You get very hard boiled eggs!

Where do chickens go to when they die?
  To oven!

Which food gets scared easily?
Chicken pie!

Why did the turkey cross the road?
To prove that he wasn't a chicken!

What do you get if you cross
a chicken with a waiter?
A hen that lays tables!

I've made the chicken soup.
*Oh, thank goodness, for a
moment I thought it was for us!*

EGGSELLENT YOLKS

These eggs are very small.
*Give them a chance, they
were only laid today!*

If you saw an egg rolling
along the road, where would
it have come from?
Why, a chicken of course!

The EGG-secutioner

DAL-EGG!

These eggs have been boiling for an hour and they're still not soft!

How can you get rid of an egg?
EGGsterminate it!

How would you beat the
biggest egg in the world?
*With the biggest egg-beater
in the world!*

There were two eggs in a pan of boiling water.
One said, "It's hot in here, isn't it?"
"Yes," replied the other egg, "but just wait
until you get out. They bash your head in
with a teaspoon!"

Why did the cook
throw the eggs away?
   They weren't all that they
   were cracked up to be!

What happened to the naughty egg?
   It was EGGspelled from school!

Why did the egg laugh?
   It heard a very funny yolk!

You have
to laugh!!

WIBBLE WOBBLE

Excuse me, did you know that
you have jelly in one ear
and custard in the other?
  *I'm sorry, you'll have to speak
  louder, I'm a trifle deaf!*

Which Italian artist wobbled?
  Botti Jelly!

What's sweet and
wobbles in the sea?
  A jelly fish!

What wobbles
by remote control?
  Jelly vision!

What happened to the sheep-dog
when it ate some jelly?
It got the collie wobbles!

Why did the jelly wobble?
Because it saw the milk shake!

What sits in a pushchair
and wobbles?
A jelly baby!

What do jelly babies
wear on their feet?
Gum boots!

How do you start
a jelly race?
Get set!

What's white, fluffy and
hangs around in trees?
  A meringue-utan!

What's white, fluffy, has
long whiskers and purrs?
  A cat-a-meringue!

How do you start a pudding race?
  Sago!

What goes round and
round in your tummy?
  Rolly-polly pudding!

Gooseberry
fool

PEA
CAN
PIE

APPLE
PUFF

What is yellow and quivers?
Cowardy custard!

What happened to the man
who stole some pudding?
He was put into custardy!

What is yellow and stupid?
Thick custard!

A chef who was making some custard,
Got himself terribly flustered,
He can't have been looking,
As he put in his cooking,
A large, rounded spoonful of mustard!

WAITER! WAITER!

"Waiter, there's a fly in my soup."

"Waiter, there's a dead fly in my soup."

SWEETIES

What is the hardest sweet of all?
  A stick of rock!

What do you call a
train full of sweets?
  A chew chew!

How can you tell when you
have had enough sugar?
  *You will feel a little
  lump in your throat!*

Leave that toffee on the floor.
  Oh, but my teef are shtill in it!

Did you like that toffee?

Mmmmmmmmmmmmm!

Your mouth looks like
a crate of old bottles.
*That's because I'm
eating wine gums!*

Why are ice-creams
like racehorses?

*Because the more
you lick 'em the
faster they go!*

LICK!

SMACK!

errk!

What is white,
furry and smells
of peppermint?
A POLO bear!

Chocolate Selection

When do you know that you have eaten all the chocolates? When the chocolate declares. (Eclairs!)

How do you stop someone eating your last chocolate? *Tie a knot in their neck!*

Where do chocolate cakes live? *In the Black Forest!*

FOOD & DRINK section

School Dinners R.E. Volting

EVEN MORE SWEETS Candy Floss

SOUPS OF THE WORLD Mister Stroney

INDIGESTION... IVOR PAIN

The Truth About School Dinners - Dean R. Bell

Italian Food Ravi-Olee

FRYING TONIGHT. OLIVE OIL

Cold Food.....Sal ADD....

VERY CHEAP MEALS NORA BONE

SAUSAGES OF THE WORLD FRANK FURTER

FILLING MEALS JANE ZEMPTY

FAST

Why don't you eat your hot dog?
I'm waiting for the mustard to cool!

There won't be any supper tonight,
I burnt something.
What did you burn?
The kitchen!

Don't eat so fast.
But I might lose my appetite!

What would you call a row of
men waiting for a haircut?
A barbecue (barber queue)!

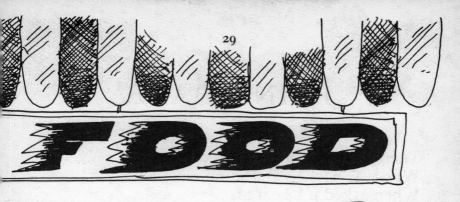

FOOD

Get me something to eat
and make it snappy.
How about a crocodile sandwich?

I have cold tongue, frog's legs
and chopped liver.
*Well, I'm very sorry for you, but
could I see the menu, please?*

What car do hot dogs drive?
Rolls!

Did you hear the story about
the ten foot long hot dog?
It takes a lot of swallowing.

BLIND DATE

There once was a well-travelled date,
Who was packed in a small, wooden crate.
When asked if he cared,
He loudly declared,
That he'd never before travelled freight.

Thought for the day

VEGGIE·TABLES

There once was a gigantic marrow,
Who had to be wheeled in a barrow.
Now he tries to forget,
That as a courgette,
He was schooled at both Eaton and Harrow!

What did the dandelion say to the vegetables?
Take me to your weeder!

How can you recognize
a parsnip?
*It has turnips at
the bottom of its
trousers!*

Which peas never get married?
Batchelor's peas!

A VEGETABLE FARM

It must have sprung a LEEK

GET IN LANE
DUAL CABBAGEWAY
↑ AHEAD ↑

V.W. BEETLE

Where had the runner bean?
To see the Brussels sprout!

What would you call
a badly behaved potato?
A common-tater!

Can an orange box?
No, but a tomato can!

What kind of dog
do you find in a
vegetable plot?
A Jack Brussel!

How can you tell when
cabbages are ripe?
  Use a green gauge!

What do you call a
potato with freckles?
  A specked-tater!

How can you recognize
a jacket potato?
  *They have big pockets
  and they're done up
  with button mushrooms!*

Why did the beetroot blush?
  *Because it saw the
  salad dressing!*

Did you hear about
the potato that
went continental?
It became a
French fry!

What is the saddest thing you
could get if you crossed a
fruit with a vegetable?
A melon-cauli!

How do we know that carrots
are good for the eyesight?
Have you ever seen a
rabbit wearing glasses?

What would you get if
you crossed an angry
dog with a lettuce?
A salad that barks!

NUTS

Which nut has no shell?
A doughnut!

So you're mad about nuts, are you?
Have you tried the nut-house!

What sort of nuts are hairy?
Chestnuts?

What is brown, wrinkly
and can see just as
well from either end?
A walnut!

Excuse me, who's in charge of the nuts?
Why, do you need taking care of?

What happened to the
nut that was beaten up?
It was an assaulted peanut!

What sort of nuts
make you sneeze?
Cashews!

What is a coconut?
*Someone who loves
their bedtime drink!*

What is brown and hairy
and wears dark glasses?
A coconut in disguise!

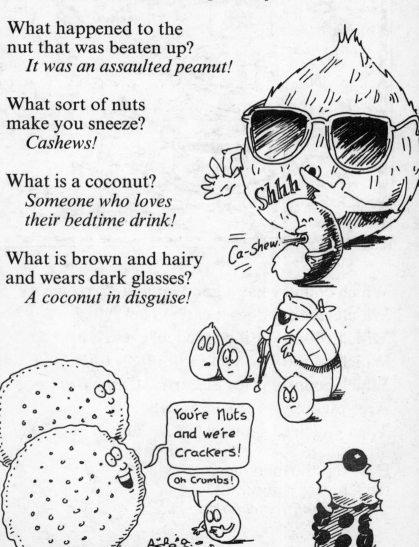

Which country has a good appetite?   *Hungary*
Which country does it eat?   *Turkey*
Which country is it cooked in?   *Greece*
Which country do you eat it off?   *China*
Which country is for dessert?   *Grape Britain*
Are you hungry?   *Yes, Siam!*
Then you need someone to . . . *Fiji!*

How did the man die in
the Chinese restaurant?
   He committed chop sueycide!

What do the French eat for breakfast?
Huit heures bix!

What is spaghetti bolognese?
Worms in tomato sauce!

What is tall and
wobbles in France?
The Trifle Tower!

What kind of cold can
you catch in Vienna?
The Schnitzels!

DOCTOR! DOCTOR!

"Doctor, I think I'm
a Cornish pasty."
  *"When did you first
  notice this complaint?"*
"Ever since I was a
sausage roll!"

"Doctor, I think
I'm a cabbage."
  *"When did you first
  notice this complaint?"*
"Ever since I
was a sprout!"

"Doctor, I think
I'm a cucumber."
  *"When did you first
  notice this complaint?"*
"Ever since I
was a gherkin!"

"Oh, Doctor, I keep
thinking that I'm
a strawberry."
  *"Well, you are
  in a jam!"*

"Doctor, I think
I'm an onion."
  *"Well, you're in
  a pickle!"*

"Doctor, I think
I'm an apple."
  *"Don't worry, I
  won't bite you!"*

"Doctor, I'm
so fed up."
  *"Then don't
  eat so much!"*

"Oh, Doctor, I'm
a little dumpling."
  *"Then don't get
  in a stew!"*

"Doctor, my family say I'm mad.
Just because I prefer long-
sleeved T-shirts."
*"But I prefer long-
sleeved T-shirts too!"*
"Oh, Doctor, that's marvellous news.
Do you like them boiled or fried?"

"Oh, Doctor, I'm boiling."
"Then just simmer down!"

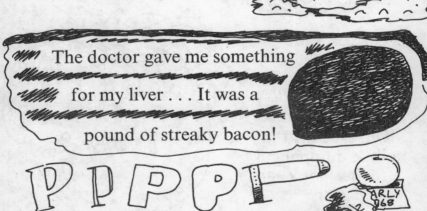

The doctor gave me something for my liver . . . It was a pound of streaky bacon!

"Doctor, my family say I'm mad.
Just because I like peas."
"But I like peas as well."
"Oh, Doctor, that's marvellous news.
Would you like to come round
and see my collection!"

Seven days of dieting make one weak. (week)

What do you call an X-ray of your stomach?
Belly vision!

What is the worst thing that a kettle can catch?
Boils!

What kind of pills get you back into shape?
Fittermin pills!

Doctor, I've got a terrible cold.

Well, you are an ice-cream!

FIT VIT PILLS

SOMETHING FISHY

What eats people two by two?
Noah's shark!

I'm on a seafood diet.
See food and I eat it!

What is the most musical fish?
The tuna!

Which fish do you find in church?
Holy mackerel!

I saw a man-eating shark at the aquarium.
Well, I saw a man eating shark in a restaurant!

IN THE KITCHEN

I bet your kitchen is clean . . .
Everything tastes of soap!

I told you to watch that pan
in case it boiled over.
*I did, it boiled over
ten minutes ago!*

What kind of tree do you
find in the kitchen?
A pantry!

Why is the cookery
teacher so special?
*Because she's in a
class of her own!*

What song would you sing
while cleaning the cooker?
Foam on the range!

Most accidents
happen in
the kitchen.

*I know . . .
I have to
eat them!*

DANGER

Why are Bs dangerous
in the kitchen?
They make oil boil!

Which chef wears
the biggest hat?
*The one with the
biggest head!*

What did the French
chef do when he saw
a girl faint?
*He gave her the
quiche of life!*

Quiche of
—life—
Take one slice
3 times a day!

Did you hear about the
chef who was so useless
that he burnt the salad?

Another chef was almost as
useless, he burnt the water!

Our water has been:
Boiled, Baked, Poached,
Fried, Basted & Steamed.

I've drunk
this water
three times
already!

What do you call a Scottish chef?
Dinner Ken!

What would you get if you crossed
a cow with three chefs?
Milk and cookies!

What is higher than a chef?
A chef's hat!

What is a bacteria?
The back of a cafeteria!

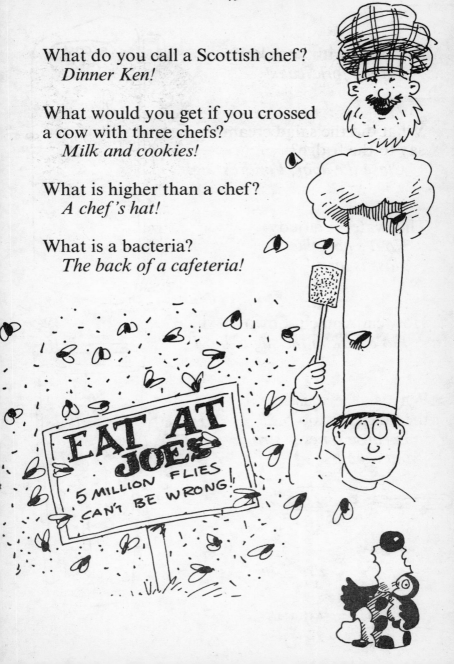

Don't eat with your knife.
  But my fork leaks!

What did the salad cream
say to the fridge?
  Close the door, I'm dressing!

This water is cloudy.
  No it's not, the
  glass is dirty!

How can you cut down on sugar?
  Put a fork in the sugar-bowl!

Why is a sieve useless if
the holes are too big?
  Because it never strains
  but it pours!

At least the glass is clean!

It's STRAINING cats and Dogs!

Who stole the fridge?
Iceburglars!

Have you filled the
salt-cellar yet?
*No, I can't get the grains
through the little hole!*

What happens if you put a
bell on the kitchen scales?
You get jingles all the weigh!

A WHALE-WEIGH
TRAIN!

What did the saucer
say to the cup?
*That's enough
of your lip!*

GULP!

the smallest
Beef-Burglar in
the world!

KNOCK! KNOCK!

Knock! Knock!
Who's there?
Arthur.
Arthur who?
Arthur any
cakes for tea?

Knock! Knock!
Who's there?
Bernadette.
Bernadette who?
Bernadette
my biscuit!

Knock! Knock!
Who's there?
Ammonia.
Ammonia who?
Ammonia the
person who
has to eat
this muck!

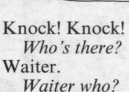

Knock! Knock!
Who's there?
Waiter.
Waiter who?
Waiter minute,
I didn't ask
for this!

Knock! Knock!
Who's there?
Irish stew.
Irish stew who?
Irish stew
in the name
of the law!

Knock! Knock!
Who's there?
Cook.
Cook who?
Is it spring
already?

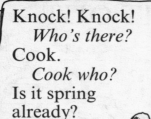

Knock! Knock!
Who's there?
Tina.
Tina who?
Tina tomatoes!

Knock! Knock!
Who's there?
Doughnut.
Doughnut who?
Doughnut
ask what's
in the pie!

Knock! Knock!
Who's there?
Felix.
Felix who?
Felix my ice-
cream I'll
bash him!

Knock! Knock!
Who's there?
Harvey.
Harvey who?
Harvey haffing
vegetables?

DISHING IT OUT

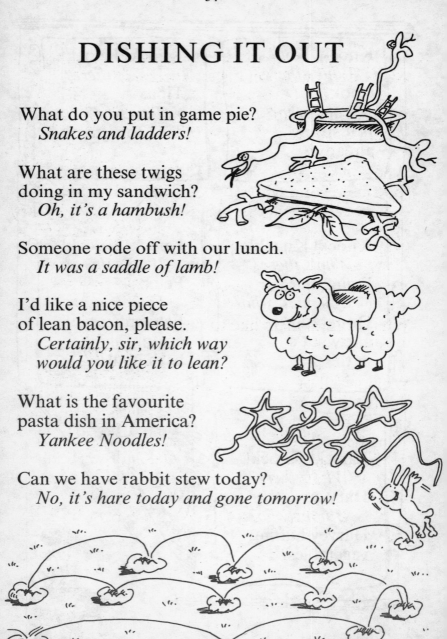

What do you put in game pie?
Snakes and ladders!

What are these twigs
doing in my sandwich?
Oh, it's a hambush!

Someone rode off with our lunch.
It was a saddle of lamb!

I'd like a nice piece
of lean bacon, please.
*Certainly, sir, which way
would you like it to lean?*

What is the favourite
pasta dish in America?
Yankee Noodles!

Can we have rabbit stew today?
No, it's hare today and gone tomorrow!

Don't touch those mashed potatoes,
your fingers will bond in two seconds!

What dish is made of tough old rats?
   Rat-a-chewy!

What do you make
solid-gold soup with?
   Twenty-two carrots!

What do scientists eat?
   *Micro chips! (They must
   be computer egg-sperts!)*

← MICRO CHIP

What do prisoners like to drink?
   Liber-tea!

What is full of
sandwiches and
calls out,
"The bells! The bells!"
   *The Lunchpack
   of Notre Dame!*

FAMOUS DISHES

F.M. Macaroni

Coq Au Van

Beef Wellington

Truncheon Meat

ASTRONAUT EATING HIS LAUNCH

KATE & SYDNEY PIE

PIE IN THE SKY

NICE PIE WITH
MY LITTLE EYE.

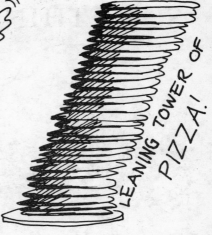

LEANING TOWER OF
PIZZA!

Toad in the hole

WELSH RABBIT.

SHARK
INFESTED
CUSTARD

SOMETHING FRUITY

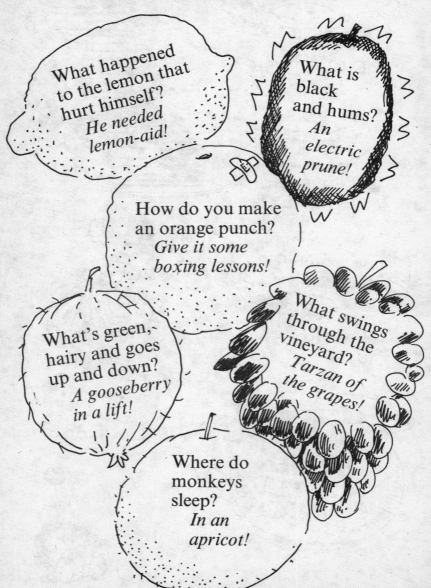

What happened to the lemon that hurt himself?
He needed lemon-aid!

What is black and hums?
An electric prune!

How do you make an orange punch?
Give it some boxing lessons!

What's green, hairy and goes up and down?
A gooseberry in a lift!

What swings through the vineyard?
Tarzan of the grapes!

Where do monkeys sleep?
In an apricot!

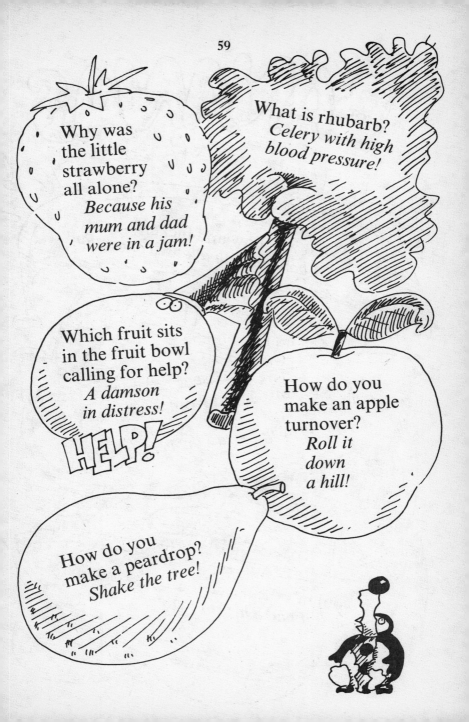

Why was the little strawberry all alone? *Because his mum and dad were in a jam!*

What is rhubarb? *Celery with high blood pressure!*

Which fruit sits in the fruit bowl calling for help? *A damson in distress!*

HELP!

How do you make an apple turnover? *Roll it down a hill!*

How do you make a peardrop? *Shake the tree!*

BANANAS

What is yellow and flickers?
A banana with a loose connection!

Why were you sacked from your job at the greengrocers?
I kept throwing away the bent bananas!

Why wouldn't the peach marry the banana?
Because it had a heart of stone!

Why don't you take the skin off that banana?
Because I know what's inside!

How do you make a banana split?
Cut it in half!

Why are you never alone with a banana?
Because they go around in bunches!

What's yellow and writes?
A ball-point banana!

Eat your greens up,
they're full of iron.
No wonder my teeth hurt!

We call our school dining-room
the Bureau of Missing Portions!

Excuse me, Miss,
there's a little
slug in my salad.
*Pass me your plate
and I'll give you
a bigger one!*

Will you eat that custard?
*I can't, the cockroaches
haven't finished bouncing
on it yet!*

BLOP

SPLAT!

What is the difference
between school dinners
and a bucket full
of pig swill?
*School dinners
come on a plate!*

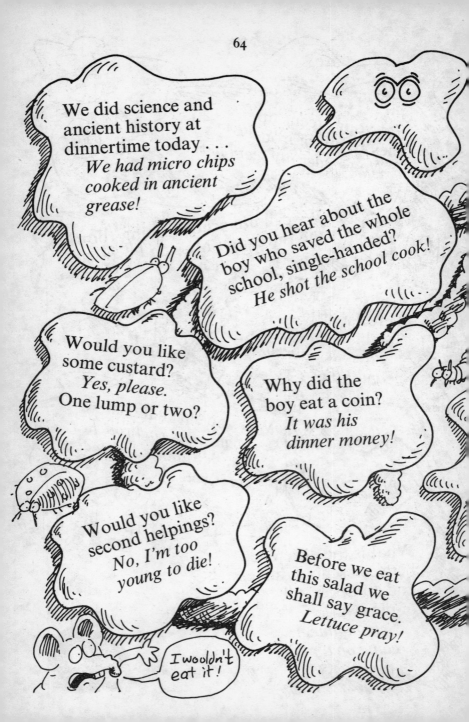

Why are you the only child in school today?
I was away yesterday so I didn't eat the school dinner!

What did the little boy say when he saw his first school dinner?
I'm off home!

Where is the best place to build the school sick-room?
Right next to the school dining-room!

Why do dinner ladies wear overalls?
So their clothes don't get spoilt when you throw bits of food at them!

Oh, sir, there's a slug on my lettuce!
Well, you did say you wanted meat!

MONSTER MUNCH AND SPOOKHETTI

There was once a vegetarian monster
who would only eat Swedes . . .
and the occasional Norwegian!

Where would a monster
go for a snack?
*Any place where
they serve people!*

What would you give
a hungry monster?
A helping hand!

What did the monster say
when he saw a traffic jam?
Mmm . . . tinned people!

What did the sea monster eat?
Fish and ships!

A monster went on a cruise. He went to the restaurant for dinner and was asked if he would like to see the menu.

"No," he replied, "just bring me the passenger list!"

What would you call a monster that ate his mother's sister?
An aunt eater!

MENU
Captains on toast

1st. Mate Salad,

Stoker Pie

Passengers with peas & Potatoes

Smoked Seadog

Steward Stew

Cabinboy Pudding.

A monster went into a restaurant and ordered the chef with a waiter on the side!

What do monsters like on their toast?
Human beans!

What would you call a sandwich man?
A monster munch!

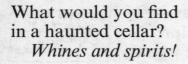

What would you find
in a haunted cellar?
Whines and spirits!

What do ghosts
like to drink?
Bier!

Why did the ghosts stop work?
To have a coffin break!

What is a ghost's
favourite meal?
Ghoulash!

What do ghosts eat
for breakfast?
Dreaded wheat!

What do you get if you cross a ghost with a packet of crisps?
A snack that goes crunch in the night!

What do Italian ghosts eat?
Spookhetti!

What is a ghost's favourite dessert?
I scream!

What do ghosts put on their cereal in the morning?
Evaporated milk!

What is a ghost's favourite sauce?
Gravey!

INVISIBLE ELEPHANTS

What is the difference between an elephant
and an apple?
   An apple is red!

What do you get if you cross an elephant with
peanut butter?
   You get a spread that never forgets!

What is the difference between an elephant and
a banana?
   *If you can't lift it it's probably a very
   heavy banana!*

Why did the elephant paint his toenails red?
   So he could hide amongst the strawberries!

Why did the elephant sit on the tomato?
   He wanted to play squash!

Why do elephants paint the soles of their feet
yellow?
   So they can hide upside down in custard!

Have you ever seen an elephant in the custard?
   Shows you what a good disguise it is!
   (Have you ever wondered what the lumps are?)

What is green and has a trunk?
An elephant that has been picked too soon!

How can you tell if there has been an elephant
in the fridge?
You will find footprints in the butter!

How can you tell if an elephant is still in the fridge?
You can't shut the door!

Why do elephants wear pink trainers?
So that they can hide in cherry trees!

How many elephants can you see?

CALL THE WAITER

"Waiter, there's a
worm on my plate."
  *"No, sir, that's the
  sausage you ordered!"*

"Waiter, I've been trying to cut
this steak for ten minutes."
  *"Well, I can't take it back now,
  sir, you've dented it!"*

"Waiter, what do you call this?"
  "It's bean soup, sir."
"I don't want to know what
it's been, what is it now?"

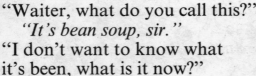

"I'll have asparagus."
  *"I'm sorry, sir, but we
  don't serve sparrows,
  and my name's not Gus!"*

"Do you serve shrimps?"
  "We serve anyone, sir!"

"Will those hamburgers be long?"
"No, sir, they'll be round!"

"How did you find your meat, sir?"
"I lifted up a pea and there it was!"

"Waiter, have you got frog's legs?"
"No, sir, it's just the way I walk!"

"Is there stew on the menu?"
*"I'm sorry, sir, I thought
I'd wiped it off!"*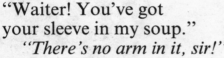

"Waiter! You've got
your sleeve in my soup."
"There's no arm in it, sir!"

SLURP! SLURP!

How does a coffee pot feel?
  Perky!

Why did you call your dog Coffee?
  Because he keeps us up all night!

What is the most useless
thing in the world?
  A waterproof tea-bag!

Is it windy?
  No, it's Thursday.
Well, let's go and have
a cup of tea then!

This coffee tastes like mud.
  *Well, it was ground only
  ten minutes ago!*

I like a nice cup of coffee in the middle of the night.

HI-BALL

RUSTY NAIL

SCREW-DRIVER

PUNCH

HARVEY WALLBANGER

FAMOUS COCKTAILS

What does a golfer drink?
Tee!

What do you get if you
cross a cow with a camel?
Lumpy milkshakes!

Which cups can't you drink from?
Buttercups and hiccups!
(*Did you know that mauve
hiccups are burple?!*)

I'd like coffee without milk, please.
*I'm sorry, sir, we're right out of
milk, would you mind if it was
without cream?*

If you haven't had a
drink for five days
you probably need a
thirst-aid kit!

LUMPY
MILKSHAKE
one hump or
two?

BREAK
GLASS IN
CASE OF
EMERGENCY

MUNCH! MUNCH!

This pancake is flat.
*Well, why don't
you recharge it?*

What happens if you eat uranium?
You'll get atomic ache!

I think that babies should
wear L plates when they eat!

Why are you eating a
circular sandwich?
*Because I like the way it
goes round in my tummy!*

How can you cure acid indigestion?
Stop drinking acid!

What's that trough doing in the corner?
That's Dad's: he eats like a horse!

That meal was awful.
  Even the dustbin has indigestion!

What should you not eat before breakfast?
  Lunch and supper!

You just don't appreciate good food.
  I would if I ever tasted any!

What happens if you eat humble pie
and talk at the same time?
  You get mumble pie!

Mum, I've made a mud pie.
  *Well, make sure you wash your
  hands before you eat it!*

The four Seasons!

You shouldn't have any more to eat. You know
it's bad to sleep on a full stomach.
That's all right, I'll sleep on my side!

What makes a good breakfast in bed?
A couple of rolls and a turnover!

What kind of food is cheeky?
Food with a lot of sauce!

The dog's eaten the dinner.
*Never mind, we'll just
have to get another dog!*

How does Batman's mother
call him in for his supper?
*Dinner, dinner, dinner,
dinner, Batman!*

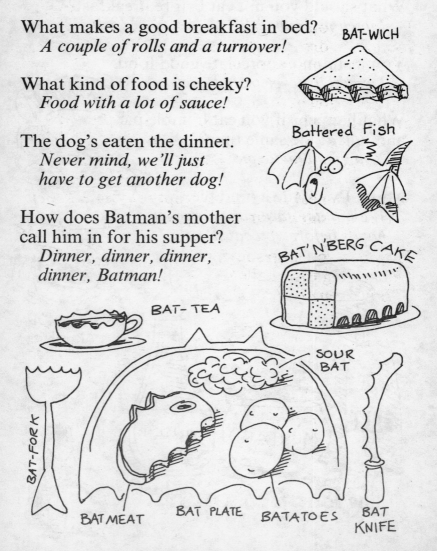

What would you like to get
your teeth into, Grandpa?
A glass of water, please!

How can you save your
food from drowning?
Send out the gravy boats!

Eat your greens, son, then you'll
grow up all big and strong.
*Oh, didn't you eat your greens
when you were a boy, Dad?*

Should you eat food on an empty stomach?
No, you should eat it off a plate.

How can you stop someone
from biting their nails?
Buy them a pair of shoes!

NOT FOR VEGETARIANS

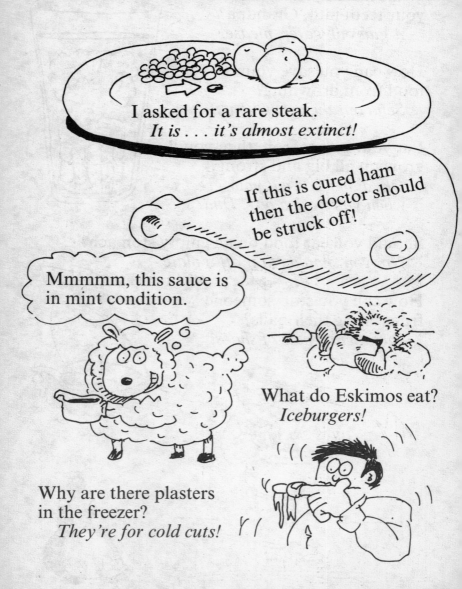

I asked for a rare steak.
It is . . . it's almost extinct!

If this is cured ham
then the doctor should
be struck off!

Mmmmm, this sauce is
in mint condition.

What do Eskimos eat?
Iceburgers!

Why are there plasters
in the freezer?
They're for cold cuts!

This chop is very tough.
*That's because it's a
karate chop!*

Ah So!

What do you call
electric mince?
A humburger!

What do you call
a pig stealer?
A ham burglar!

RARE
STEAK

When is steak
very expensive?
When it's rare!

CRACKIE
CRACKIE

Why is pork like
an old radio?
*Because they
both have a lot
of crackling!*

SOUPERTIME

What goes: AJDH BIAKAGISLURP?
Someone eating alphabet soup!

"Waiter, this bowl is wet."
"No, that's your soup, sir!"

What would you call Mr Campbell?
Soup-er-man!

Faster than a speeding noodle!

There's something funny about this soup.
Then why aren't you laughing?

This is very funny soup, how did you make it?
I used laughing stock!

SOUP

What is a vampire's
favourite brand of soup?
Bat-chelors!

"Mum, what's a vampire?"
*"Be quiet and eat
your soup before
it clots!"*

What is a vampire's
favourite soup?
Scream of tomato!

Which soup gets
scared out of
its noodles?
Chicken soup!

MILKSOPS

Where does margarine come from?
Imitation cows!

What is full of milk and
only has one horn?
The milk lorry!

How do the Welsh eat cheese?
Very Caerphilly!

What is yellow, green and hairy?
*The piece of cheese that fell
down behind the cooker last year!*

I don't like the cheese
with holes in it.
*Then leave the holes on
the side of the plate, dear!*

What do you call Eskimo money?
Iced lolly!

Did you know that they make a
cheese that is so smelly that no
one can get near enough to eat it!

What is Cheddar Gorge?
A cheese-eating contest!

Did you hear about the cat that
won the milk-drinking contest?
It lapped the field!

Why do you have such
tiny tea-cups?
*Because we can only
get condensed milk!*

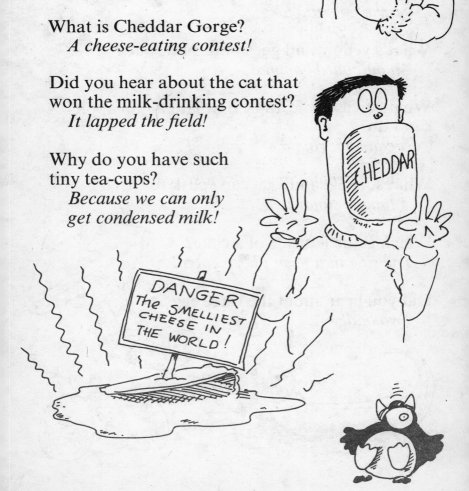

GRIDDLES

What is the difference between a hungry person and a greedy person?
A hungry person longs to eat while a greedy person eats too long!

What's yellow and goes putt, putt, putt?
An outboard banana!

What can a whole apple do that half an apple can't do?
It can look round!

What sort of sandwich can speak for itself?
A tongue sandwich!

Which is the left side of a cake?
The side that hasn't been eaten!

Did you hear about the three eggs?
Two bad!

Can an apple turnover?
   No, but I saw a cheese dip!

Can a salad bowl?
   No, but I saw a lunch box!

What is the best way to stop food going off?
   Eat it quick!

Why must you never put the
letter M into the fridge?
   Because it turns ice to mice!

What is wet and crunchy?
   A water biscuit!

What food is good for the brain?
   Noodle soup!

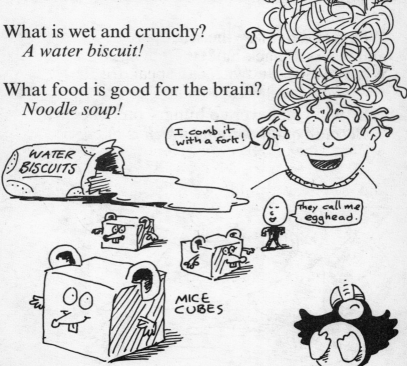

Why is milk like long-distance running?
Because it strengthens the calves!

What would you call a midnight feast?
A bed-spread!

How many peas are there in a pound?
There's only one "P" in pound!

Is it possible to live on garlic alone?
*Well, you don't think anyone will come
close, do you!*

What food lives by the sea
and wears a black hat?
A sand witch!

Why will you never go hungry on the beach?
Because of all the sand which is there!

What is the difference between
a lolly and a stamp?
*One you lick and stick,
the other's a lick on a stick!*

What is the hardest thing to cook?
Well, scrambled eggs take a lot of beating!

If can't is short for cannot
what is don't short for?
Doughnut!

Why is the Yorkshire cricket team
like a Yorkshire pudding?
Because they both rely on good batters!

Why is a boy scout like a frozen dinner?
Because they're both prepared!

Where do spies shop?
At a snopermarket!

FRYER TUCK

Which friar cooks potatoes?
The chip monk!

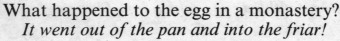

What happened to the egg in a monastery?
It went out of the pan and into the friar!

When do they have eggs and
bacon in a monastery?
On a Friar Day!

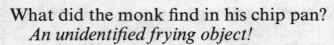

What did the monk find in his chip pan?
An unidentified frying object!

What do you call the chief sausage?
A head banger!

What do you call a sausage's photo call?
Bangers and flash!

Why are sausages so disgusting?
Because they spit!

What is the noisiest food?
Clangers and bash!

I'm the Griller!

A BUN DANCE

Why don't you pick up that bag of flour?
Because it's self-raising!

Why are bakers stupid?
Because they sell what they knead!

What sound does unleavened bread make?
Pitta patta!

What sort of bread is stupid?
Half-baked bread!

Why do bakers go to work?
To earn an honest crust!

flour for Angel Cakes!

Why didn't anyone recognize the biscuit?
Because it had been a wafer too long!

What biscuits do
idiots like?
Crackers!

What did the biscuit say
when it was run over?
Oh, crumbs!

A WAFER IN
DISGUISE

What do you call a
clever biscuit?
A smart cookie!

What sort of
biscuit talks
a lot?
A waffle!

Waffle,
Waffle,
Drivel,
Drivel,
Claptrap!

Pin-wheel biscuit

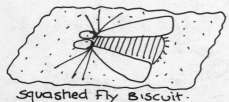

Squashed Fly Biscuit.

Jammy,
Jolly,
Roger,
Dodger!

THE LAST SLICE

What is yellow and
jumps from cake to cake?
Tarzipan!

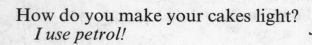

How do you make your cakes light?
I use petrol!

These cakes are awful.
*But the recipe says
they're delicious!*

Which part of a cake
does the dentist make?
The filling!

Which cake is not nice to eat?
A cake of soap!

MARBLE
CAKE

You're getting old when the candles
cost more than the cake!

What cake makes you choke?
Coughee cake!

What are the two heaviest cakes?
Rock cake and marble cake!

What sort of cakes do elves eat?
Fairy cakes!

What is the best thing
to put into a cake?
Your teeth!

How do you make a Swiss roll?
Push her down the hill!

Coughee
Cake

Fairy Cake.

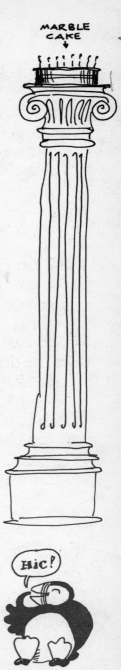

Hic!

How do you know
when a Midnight
feast is over?

Your torch battery
runs out!